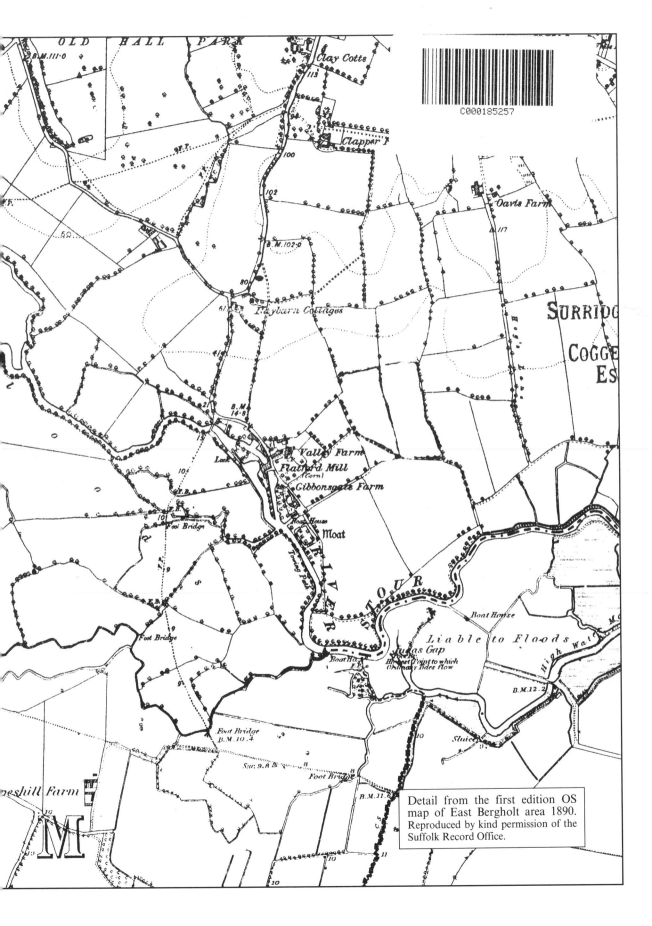

Detail from the first edition OS map of East Bergholt area 1890. Reproduced by kind permission of the Suffolk Record Office.

# Dedham, Flatford & East Bergholt

## A Pictorial History

Willy Lott's Cottage, from Flatford Mill. Constable's friend and biographer, C.R. Leslie, wrote of the cottage that Willy Lott 'passed more than eighty years without having spent four whole days away from it'.

# Dedham, Flatford & East Bergholt

## A Pictorial History

## Ian Yearsley

## Phillimore

1996

Published by
PHILLIMORE & CO. LTD.
Shopwyke Manor Barn, Chichester, West Sussex

ISBN 1 86077 010 X

Printed and bound in Great Britain by
BIDDLES LTD.
Guildford, Surrey

*This book is dedicated to Michael Guy and family.*
*Thank you for giving me the opportunity to prove myself.*

# List of Illustrations

*Frontispiece:* Willy Lott's Cottage, from Flatford Mill

# *Acknowledgements*

The author wishes to thank the following for permission to reproduce photographs and illustrations: Derek Chapman, 10, 24, 26, 130, 131, 140-47, 159, 160, 165-68, 172; East Bergholt Society, 80, 90, 91, 148-50, 152-54, 156, 157, 162-64; Essex Record Office, 18; Paul Gallifant/Dedham Vale Society, 31, 49, 158, 169-71; John Marriage/River Stour Trust, 42-45, 108, 109, 115, 123-26; Suffolk Record Office, 76, 89, 92, 98, 104, 151, 161, 174, 176. The remainder are from the author's collection.

In addition to the acknowledgements given above, I would particularly like to thank Jessica Bishop, Derek Chapman, Paul Gallifant and John Marriage for their time and assistance in helping me to select photographs for inclusion in this book.

Further thanks for various types of assistance go to Beaulieu Motor Museum, Brenda & Bue at Old Hall, Celia Richardson of the Dedham Vale & Stour Valley Countryside Project, Essex Libraries, the Essex Record Office, Keith Turner and the National Trust, the Office of Population, Censuses and Surveys (OPCS), Suffolk Libraries, the Suffolk Record Office, Jonkheer P. Quarles van Ufford, Wardle Storeys and Patricia Wright.

Thanks also to everyone at Phillimore who was involved with the production of this book and to my wife, Alison, for her encouragement and support.

# *Introduction*

## Topography

Dedham, East Bergholt and Flatford are situated in the Stour Valley on the Essex-Suffolk border. Dedham is in Essex; East Bergholt and Flatford are in Suffolk. Forming a triangle of settlements, each barely a mile from the other two, they occupy the central section of that part of the valley which is known as Dedham Vale, an area made famous by the landscape painter, John Constable, and now a popular destination for day-trippers.

The River Stour, which runs through the Vale, forms the border between Essex and Suffolk, as it once did between the Saxons and the Angles. As with other rivers on the east coast, the Stour was used as a method of transport from the earliest times and was consequently an important access route to inland areas for invading armies from overseas. Later it became an essential component of the area's transport network and in that capacity it helped to sustain much of the trade of the villages and towns of north Essex and south Suffolk.

The town of Dedham grew up on the valley floor immediately to the south of the river. Covering approximately 3 miles by 2.5 miles and encompassing some 2,500 acres, Dedham parish is bounded by the Stour in the north, the London-Ipswich road at Stratford St Mary in the west, the Shirburn Brook at Flatford in the east and Dedham Heath and the much reduced adjacent woodland in the south.

The village of East Bergholt grew up on a hill on the north side of the valley downstream from Dedham, while Flatford, little more than a hamlet, was established nearby on the Stour's northern bank. East Bergholt parish, which now includes Flatford, covers about 3,000 acres and is bounded in the south by the Stour, stretching north as far as Lattinford.

The total population of the three settlements is probably four thousand.

Since the 1960s, the whole area has been declared an Area of Outstanding Natural Beauty (AONB) and parts of Dedham and East Bergholt have been designated conservation areas. Flatford, which contains the most concentrated grouping of Grade I listed buildings in the locality, is owned by the National Trust.

## Early History of Dedham

There was definitely a settlement at Dedham in Saxon times and there may even have been one there during the Roman occupation. The name derives from the Saxon 'Dydda's Ham'—the settlement of Dydda's people. There was formerly a ford to the east of Dedham Mill, which was the lowest point at which the river could normally be crossed—the ford at nearby Flatford was often covered by floods and spring tides and there were no bridges in the area then.

Dedham village grew up at the junction of the River Stour and its tributary, the Black Brook, which still runs through somewhat canalised channels in the town. The water of the Black Brook was actually very clear and the name is thought to derive from either the French word, *blanc*, for 'white', or the German word from which we get 'bleach'. The settlement was set back from the Stour to avoid the regular flooding which occurred and was located far enough away from the main Colchester-Harwich Roman road to escape any trouble.

The Stour was always the larger of the two watercourses and there was a mill here in 1086 at the time of the Domesday Survey, when the population of Dedham (recorded, apparently by mistake, as 'Delham') was approximately two hundred. There were also fishponds in the lower reaches of the Black Brook at this time.

The original Manor House and Farm were located at the east end of the churchyard, where Royal Square today faithfully retains the square farmyard shape around which the Hall and the farm buildings were located. The main road out of the town was to the east to Colchester, along what is now Brook Street but which was once called the King's Highway. There was no road-bridge by the mill and the roads to the west to Colchester and Stratford St Mary were both developed later.

The Hall stood at the west of the square, hard up against the churchyard wall. The south side of the yard was used for farm offices, sheds and barns, of which the surviving Duchy Barn—now home to the tourist information centre and named after a subsequent local landowner, the Duchy of Lancaster—is a reminder. On the east were the stables, byres and dairy. The north side of the square was open—the lane opposite leading down to the Stour and Dedham Mill.

Behind the Duchy Barn were the south fields of the manor farm, a name which is preserved in the early 16th-century 'Flemish Houses' of Southfields, across the playing fields behind the church. The once extensive woodland beyond the fields contributed timber for building, fuel for fires and beechmast for pigs.

The earliest houses in Dedham were grouped around the long-disappeared village green, formerly situated where the High Street meets Princel Lane. This area later became the market place and in its heyday the weekly Tuesday market stretched from the *Sun Hotel* to the *Marlborough Head*. The wide street where the market was held is still a feature of the town.

At the time of the Domesday Survey, the manor of Dedham was owned by Roger of Ramis (or Raismes), whose descendants held the land for some 300 years. In 1240, however, at the hands of Sir John de Stuteville (one of Roger's descendants), the manor was partitioned, with much of the land to the north east of the High Street (i.e. towards Flatford) being given to Campsey Priory in Suffolk. The job of providing a clergyman for Dedham was given to Butley Abbey (until the Dissolution, when it passed to the Duchy of Lancaster). Although the original Manor House has gone, the hall of the Campsey Manor, now called Dedham Hall but shown on some old maps as Netherhall, survives.

In 1337 the original manor land was given by the Crown, to whom it had reverted on the death of Ramis' last direct descendant, to Robert Ufford, Earl of Suffolk. He is thought to have provided an archery field, at the bend in Brook Street where a path extends across the fields to Flatford.

In 1381 the land came into the possession of Michael de la Pole, Chancellor to Richard II, who introduced an annual three-day fair in 1383 to stimulate trade and probably provided land and milling facilities for struggling local cloth manufacturers.

One other subsequent Dedham landholder worthy of note was Sir John Fastolf, victor in the 14th-century 'Battle of the Herrings' against the French (so-called because he was defending the army's provisions) and apparently later the butt of Shakespeare's humour as the character Falstaff.

## Early History of East Bergholt and Flatford

There may well have been a Roman settlement at East Bergholt, as traces of an apparently Roman burial ground have been found in the area, and there would also seem to have been a degree of Anglo-Saxon occupation. At the time of the Norman Conquest, 'Bercolt' was a Royal manor, held by King Harold, and was the largest and most important settlement in this part of Suffolk. Its name is thought most likely to derive from its geographical location in a 'wooded hill' or 'birch grove'.

'Bercolt' actually grew up as a number of separate settlements around a central area of common land. This land was never subsequently developed to any great extent and the shape of the village today preserves the original layout, although the common land itself was eventually enclosed as a result of the Enclosure Acts of the early 19th century.

Over the succeeding centuries the old Royal manor became divided into four separate manors—Old Hall, Spencers, Illaries and St John's (sometimes known as The Commandery). Old Hall was the principal manor and was the scene of an uprising during the Peasants' Revolt of 1381, when all the manorial rolls were stolen and burnt in a public ceremony in front of the church. At this time the manor was owned by Sir John de Sutton, but in 1425 it passed, by marriage, into the hands of the de Vere family, Earls of Oxford and major landowners at other nearby places such as Castle Hedingham in Essex. It was eventually sold out of the family in 1579.

The manor of St John's was the last surviving part of the old Royal manor and was given by Henry II to the Knights Templar, from whom it passed to the Knights Hospitaller (the Knights of St John of Jerusalem) and became attached to their Commandery at Battisford (hence the alternative name). At the Dissolution, the manor was given to the de Veres and it, too, was then sold out of the family in 1579.

The manors of Spencers and Illaries were sub-manors of St John's and are thought to have been named after local families—the Spencers and the St Hilarys. They were probably in existence as separate manors before about 1290.

The origins of Flatford are less well documented than those of East Bergholt, though it is thought that an early, possibly Roman, settlement grew up there at the lowest regularly fordable point on the river (Dedham was fordable at all times, Flatford most of the time, Cattawade, even further downriver, only at low tide). This location would probably have been chosen partly to protect areas further inland from invasion by river and partly to guard the crossing point.

It is also thought that there was once a much larger settlement at Flatford than there is today and that, for reasons uncertain, the community moved up the hill to East Bergholt. A celebrated map of the area by William Brasier (1731) shows a 'Church Field' and an 'Old Parsonage' at Flatford, which implies that there was once a church there. With its river frontage, mill and river crossing facilities it could well have been an important early settlement.

Until 1855 the living of the church of East Bergholt was shared with that of neighbouring Brantham, so that the churches of the two villages were looked after by the same vicar. The parishes were separated in that year following the death of Reverend Joshua Rowley, who disposed of the advowson to Emmanuel College, Cambridge, which chose to appoint separate vicars.

In the late 19th century the 130-acre Brooklands Farm at Brantham was chosen as the site for a new xylonite factory (a product similar to celluloid). The factory subsequently became a major employer for both Brantham and East Bergholt residents and new houses were also built locally to accommodate workers moving to the area. Brantham was chosen because of its proximity to good rail and water communications —the factory did not have to rely exclusively on one method of transportation.

## Agriculture and the Cloth Industry

Both Dedham and East Bergholt, like much of the rest of the eastern counties, owed their early livelihood to the success of local agriculture. Arable farming, pasture land and wildfowl breeding are all listed amongst the early types of agriculture in Dedham Vale, where the wide, flat, riverside meadows that stretched from Stratford to Flatford and beyond offered ideal terrain for cattle and sheep farming in particular. Cheese and dairy products were manufactured in the area, but the most important by-product of local livestock farming was its rôle in the development of the cloth industry, which was ultimately to rival agriculture as the chief source of income in Essex and Suffolk and become an important national, and even international, industry.

In the early days of the industry, the coarse wool of local sheep was simply sent abroad for others to make into garments. Monastic houses, in particular, were heavily involved in the export of wool to places such as Italy and Flanders. For Dedham, East Bergholt and Flatford the River Stour was an essential communications channel, providing access by water both to the London markets and to ports like Harwich, from where wool could be exported.

In the 14th century, however, when France threatened to annexe Flanders, Edward III banned the export of wool and the import of foreign-made cloth in an attempt to encourage the establishment of a cloth manufacturing industry at home and also to encourage leading Flemish weavers to bring their skills to England. The Flemish, who arrived predominantly through the east-coast ports of Harwich and Ipswich, began to settle in the towns of north Essex and south Suffolk, bringing with them new skills and techniques which were to give a fresh impetus to the growing English cloth industry.

With the nearby towns of Colchester and Ipswich beginning to profit from the skills of these new arrivals, surrounding towns and villages were quick to realise the benefits of entering into this rapidly growing industry for themselves. Both Dedham and East Bergholt had good road links to the two towns, ready access to the sea, their own mills, good water supplies (essential for cleaning the raw material) and, most importantly, vast numbers of sheep, doubled in Dedham by the Normans in their first 20 years of local occupation. Over the next 300 years, hundreds of local people became involved in the industry—as shepherds, dyers, spinners, weavers or cloth traders—and new houses began to spring up in both communities.

The industry reached its peak in the 15th and 16th centuries and much of the wealth generated by the clothiers who oversaw the entire cloth production process—from the back of the sheep to the distribution of the finished item—was ploughed back into the local community. At Dedham, the construction of the magnificent church of

St Mary (built 1492-1519) was financed almost entirely by the leading local cloth merchants.

In the 16th century, however, the industry began to decline and the unfinished tower of the church of St Mary at East Bergholt (dating from c.1525) gives an indication of the differing fortunes of local businessmen even on opposite sides of the same valley and also shows how rapidly the industry began to decline once decay had set in.

The permanent collapse of the local cloth industry was, however, delayed somewhat by the influx of Dutch refugees fleeing persecution on the Continent, who settled at Colchester and brought with them their own techniques and several new materials. These new products—finer cloths such as bays, says and perpetuanas—became known as the New Draperies, replacing what were consequently called the Old Draperies, and there was much resistance to the newcomers from those employed in the older branch of the industry. Nevertheless, the creation of the Dutch Bay Hall at Colchester led to that town becoming a focal point for the distribution of finished products from north Essex and south Suffolk and much of the cloth from Dedham in particular passed through it.

An inherent problem in this early industry was, however, that it was virtually all domestic. Work was farmed out to individuals to perform in their own homes and there was very little mechanisation, with no real factories in either Dedham or East Bergholt. As the Industrial Revolution began to gather pace in the north, where the textile industry was starting anew, with new factories, new inventions and ready access to coalfields to power the new machinery, the cloth industry in Essex and Suffolk began to suffer irretrievably. The influx of better and cheaper cloth from abroad, war with Spain (one of the area's best customers), a ban on the export of undyed cloth and the 1648 Siege of Colchester also had their effects—and when the New Draperies themselves began to decline, in the latter half of the 17th century, there was no new impetus from abroad to keep them afloat. Even legislation requiring the dead to be buried in woollen shrouds did little to stave off the industry's inevitable collapse.

In 1734 John Kirby wrote of East Bergholt in his *The Suffolk Traveller* that 'cloth manufacture formerly flourished here... [but] the town is greatly reduced, many houses having lately been pulled down'. Of Dedham, Philip Morant could write in his *History and Antiquities of the County of Essex* in 1768 that the bay trade was 'greatly upon the decline'.

In some areas of Essex and Suffolk silk manufacture did its best to keep the cloth industry alive into the 19th century, but it was with the close of the 18th century that the industries in Dedham and East Bergholt really died. Fortunately for both places, they still had agriculture to fall back on.

With a return to agriculture, cereal crops became the most commonly farmed in East Bergholt, especially barley, which was shipped downriver to the maltings in the estuary at Mistley. Golding Constable, father of John, was a prosperous corn and coal merchant at East Bergholt, Flatford and Dedham in the late 18th and early 19th centuries.

Despite agricultural depression towards the end of the 19th century and, at about the same time, the closure of East Bergholt windmill (which Golding Constable once owned along with Dedham and Flatford Mills), the whole area remained largely agricultural and retains a farmland appearance to this day, despite some residential expansion at East Bergholt in particular.

## Religion

While the cloth industry was reaching its peak in Essex and Suffolk, a wind of religious change was blowing through the country. In the 16th century, with the severance of religious ties with Rome and the growth of the Church of England, more importance was being placed on the giving of sermons in church.

Initially such preaching was banned because it was feared that it would lead to civil unrest and only official doctrines were allowed to be read out. This prompted local people to employ their own preachers—known as lecturers—to give out the message they wanted. In Dedham and East Bergholt, which were strongly Protestant, the use of lecturers became a major component of religious affairs and the lecturer often worked alongside the vicar to deliver the religious message. At Dedham, which was the acknowledged local centre of Protestantism, a lecture was held on market day, which had the added bonus of bringing into the town people whose purchases would help to prop up the flagging cloth trade.

Prominent Dedham lecturers included Edmund Chapman (lecturer c.1577-1602), John Rogers (1605-36), Matthew Newcomen (1636-62) and William Burkitt (1692-1703), while East Bergholt had the even longer-serving Dr. William Jones (vicar 1591-1633 and also lecturer for part of this time). Rogers, in particular, spoke with such passion that up to 1,200 people at a time attended his lectures and new galleries had to be erected in the church. He became known from his oratorical style as 'Roaring Rogers' and at his funeral 'there were more people than three such churches could hold'. The Dedham Lectureship was finally ended in 1918, when it was combined with the role of vicar.

The Puritan element in Dedham was so strong that it even extended overseas: Dedham inhabitants, including members of the Sherman family who were to become ancestors of the famous General W.T. Sherman, helped to found one of the first towns in the New World—Dedham, Massachussetts.

Both Dedham and East Bergholt were also, not surprisingly, home to major Non-Conformist gatherings; a Dissenters' Chapel was established in East Bergholt as early as 1689 and a similar building appeared in Dedham some 50 years later. Even earlier still, Robert Samuell of East Bergholt had been burned at the stake in 1555 for refusing to renounce his religious beliefs.

In more recent centuries, East Bergholt was also home to a Benedictine convent, which operated from the former manor house of Old Hall between 1856 and 1940. The nuns added several extensions to the structure (the original manor house had by now been replaced) and opened a small chapel to the public. In 1909 the community was rocked by scandal when one of their number, Margaret Mary Moult, 'escaped' from the convent when she could no longer bear the strict regime that operated there. Her story, 'The Escaped Nun', was published by Cassell in 1911.

During the Second World War, Old Hall was used as an army base, but from 1946 to 1973 it was home to another religious order, that of a Franciscan friary. It is now occupied by a community housing association.

## Schools

During the period of cloth industry prosperity, both Dedham and East Bergholt were also fortunate to be endowed with schools by local benefactors.

At about the same time that the Lectureship was set up in Dedham, two schools were also established in the town. The Grammar School (later known as the Royal Grammar School) was founded by Dame Joan Clarke, with an endowment from the will of William Littlebury, in 1571. It was given a charter in 1575 and closed only as recently as 1889. The English School (now known as Sherman's) was set up by the wealthy clothier, Edmund Sherman, in 1599 and lasted until 1872.

The grammar school provided education for up to 20 boys in classical subjects such as Latin and Greek grammar (hence the name), whilst the English school provided for the education of perhaps 16 boys in the three 'Rs'. Both schools took boarders, who lived in the respective attics.

The first reference to a school in East Bergholt dates from 1584, though it was apparently not until 1594 that the first proper school building was erected, under the auspices of Mrs. Lettice Dykes, with financial assistance from Edward Lambe, Lord of the Manors of Spencers and Illaries. This building, still known as the Lambe School, survives to this day, being used, following restoration in the 1980s, as a hall for public functions.

As awareness of the need for proper schooling grew, the Lambe School was eventually replaced in 1831 by a new boys' school at Burnt Oak, one of the originally separate settlements from which East Bergholt had grown up. After this, the Lambe School was used exclusively for girls.

In the 1870s, when new education legislation made it compulsory for local authorities to provide schooling for local children (it had been optional until this time), the Burnt Oak building was expanded and the girls were also accommodated on the site. The Lambe School was used only for Sunday School, though it was later a Council meeting room.

Eventually Burnt Oak School itself was replaced—by a new primary school building in 1966. Burnt Oak School has since been demolished. East Bergholt now also has a high school, whose catchment area covers many of the surrounding villages.

## The Social Scene

The success of the early schools in Dedham and East Bergholt meant that wealthy families were lured to the area by the promise of a good education for their sons (girls were not taught in the early days). The money they brought with them helped to prop up the local economy and reduce the impact of decline that the cloth industry had left behind it. It also helped to employ, as servants, some of the otherwise unemployed locals. John Glyde, in his *Suffolk in the 19th Century*, wrote that East Bergholt was 'striking proof of the value of a resident gentry to poor inhabitants of a village'.

The wealthy also brought with them an image of affluence that helped to continue the atmosphere of financial security that the rich local clothiers had originally created. In the late 18th and early 19th centuries Dedham in particular was home to a thriving local social scene, the Dedham Ball attracting the top people from miles around. In 1818 the only comparable rival attractions in the area were said to be the balls at Bury St Edmunds and Bocking and people were coming from as far afield as Wivenhoe, on the other side of Colchester, to attend. Music, dancing and eating were the prime pastimes; no alcohol was permitted, but there were card tables. The Dedham Ball lasted until about the 1870s but had passed its peak some decades before that.

Other top social pastimes such as rowing competitions, cricket, bowls and quoits all took place in Dedham, while East Bergholt also had its own society attractions. All these activities helped to establish both settlements as popular places of residence for the fairly wealthy—a tradition which continues to this day.

**The Stour Navigation**

The River Stour had always been an important amenity for Dedham and East Bergholt, whether it be as a route of transportation, a power source for milling or a water source for the washing of wool. Gradually, more and more industries began to rely on the waterway for transportation of goods and in 1705 an Act was passed to make the river navigable from its estuary at Manningtree to the Suffolk town of Sudbury, over twenty miles inland.

Sudbury had itself been an important cloth town and possessed a number of other industries, such as brick-making and brewing, which relied upon the river for transport. Other important commodities which came to be transported downriver included barley, bricks, butter, clover-seed, malt, oil, paper, pitch and wheat, whilst coal, marl and London night-soil were carried in the other direction from the Manningtree and Mistley quays. Many of the old riverside cloth mills on the Stour were converted to accommodate these replacement industries.

The 1705 Act was one of the earliest such acts in the country and the river consequently became a busy commercial waterway, with dozens of horse-drawn barges plying their trade up and down the Stour Valley. The journey from Manningtree to Sudbury took about two days because of the number of locks that had to be negotiated and also because the towpath ran in sections on alternate sides of the river, so that the barge horses themselves had to be transported across the river each time the towpath changed sides. The first of John Constable's famous six-foot paintings, 'The White Horse' (1819), shows just such an activity taking place.

'The White Horse' was one of many such river scenes to be captured on canvas by Constable, whose family played an active part in ensuring the effective operation of the waterway and the maintenance of towpaths and lockgates. The artist's father, Golding, and two relatives of another famous Suffolk painter, Thomas Gainsborough, were later Commissioners of the Stour Navigation—the body set up to oversee the smooth running of the venture.

The Stour Navigation flourished for some 200 years before the growth of the railways—quicker and cheaper than waterborne transport—began to make a dent in the profits and the number of barges using the waterway began to decline. Some local people still used the waterway to row to the nearest railway station, at Manningtree, but it had begun to close to commercial traffic, despite remaining in use for commercial purposes as far upriver as Dedham Mill until the early 1930s. The most important commercial use for the river today is for the abstraction of water to serve the population in the comparatively drier areas of south Essex.

Although the commercial use of the river has gone (unless one counts the pleasure boats for hire at Dedham and Flatford), the public right of navigation of the Stour remains and the River Stour Trust actively campaigns to keep the waterway open for leisure and recreational pursuits.

## John Constable

The countryside around Dedham, East Bergholt and Flatford was made famous in the late 18th and early 19th centuries through the pictures of the landscape painter, John Constable.

Constable was born in East Bergholt in 1776. His father owned a considerable amount of land and property in Bergholt itself and also, at various stages, ran nearby Flatford, Dedham and Brantham Mills. The family home, East Bergholt House, was built by Golding in the centre of the village just a few years before John was born, but was demolished in the 1840s.

The young Constable was educated at the Royal Grammar School in Dedham and his daily walk to school took him through some delightful countryside landscapes—landscapes which were later to be immortalised in his sketches and paintings.

Constable died in 1837 and is best remembered today for his large oil paintings—'The Haywain' (1821) and 'The Cornfield' (1826) being his most popular. He acknowledged the rôle that the Stour Valley scenery played in his development with the oft-quoted phrase: 'these scenes made me a painter'. He captured them so accurately on canvas that even during his lifetime the area became known as 'Constable Country'.

In the 20th century Dedham has been home to two other artists of national repute: Sir Alfred Munnings, president of the Royal Academy of Art in the 1940s and famous for his horse paintings and controversial views, and Tom Keating, whose 'copies' of the Old Masters, including some Constables, were difficult to tell apart from the originals. Munnings' Dedham home, Castle House, is now a museum of his work; a copy of Keating's painting of 'The Haywain in Reverse' hangs in the Granary Museum at Flatford.

## Recent History: Tourism & Conservation

It was largely through Constable's paintings that Dedham Vale became known outside its immediate locality. His biographer, C.R. Leslie, drew attention to the area through his *Memoirs of the Life of John Constable* (1843), when writing with astonishment, after the artist's death, of his own first visit to Flatford with some friends.

'We found [he wrote] that the scenery of eight or ten of our late friend's most important subjects might be enclosed by a circle of a few hundred yards at Flatford, very near Bergholt; within this space are the lock which forms the subject of several pictures—Willy Lott's House—the little raised wooden bridge and the picturesque cottage near it... and the meadow in which the picture of "Boatbuilding" was entirely painted. So startling was the resemblance of some of these scenes to the pictures of them, which we knew so well, that we could hardly believe we were for the first time standing on the ground from which they were painted.'

By the 20th century Dedham Vale had become a mecca for countless other artists and large numbers of tourists and the pressure to develop Dedham and, in particular, East Bergholt, especially after the war, began to grow. A succession of post-war development applications, all vigorously fought by local people—including Sir Alfred Munnings, who even financed some local conservation projects from his own money—led to a government-commissioned report into the future of the Vale.

The outcome was the declaration of Dedham Vale as an Area of Outstanding Natural Beauty (AONB) and the placing of a restriction on new development in Dedham,

East Bergholt, Flatford and the surrounding areas. Parts of Dedham and East Bergholt were also designated as conservation areas and numerous important buildings at all three locations were listed, some as high as Grade I. The area is now also designated an Environmentally Sensitive Area (ESA), a scheme which encourages farmers to use traditional grazing methods throughout the Vale.

Long before this, the National Trust had already begun to acquire buildings and farmland around Flatford, starting in the 1920s with a generous gift from Thomas Parkington, and bit by bit the whole Vale was coming under an umbrella of protection. The River Stour Trust, the Dedham Vale Society, the East Bergholt Society, the Field Studies Council, the local authorities and others all now do their bit to help to protect the Vale.

As with all natural tourist attractions, however, a balance has to be struck. Tourists are welcomed and facilities are provided for their use and they, in return, are expected to respect the places that they visit and leave them for others to enjoy in centuries to come. For there is one thing about this area that is certain: with its history, charm and beautiful landscapes, Dedham Vale will *always* be a mecca for tourists and artists and visitors from overseas.

# Dedham—Village Centre

**1** Dedham High Street from an engraving of 1832, re-published as a postcard by the photographer, F. Artis, who had a business in Dedham in the years before the First World War. St Mary's church was a regular feature in Constable's paintings. The big building on the left is the Royal Grammar School, which Constable attended. The inn on the right is the *Marlborough Head*, whose sign was once painted by Constable's friend, John Dunthorne.

**2** A similar view of Dedham High Street from slightly further back than in the previous picture, with St Mary's church and, on the extreme left, the Congregational Church, visible through the trees. This was originally the main route into Dedham village centre, the road leading into the High Street being known initially as the King's Highway and more recently as Brook Street. Canon G.H. Rendall, writing in 1937, reported that 'Dedham, first a hamlet, then a small country town, has passed into the condition of a thriving residential village'.

**3** A similar photo, but from the 1950s. More vehicles have appeared in the street and the pavements have been made-up, but a pram stands, by coincidence, in almost exactly the same spot as in the previous picture. The cottages mark the junction of Brook Street with the High Street, which widens noticeably just beyond them.

**4** A classic view of Dedham High Street from a similar viewpoint to the first picture. The main difference between this scene and a similar view today is the complete absence of traffic—Dedham is now a major tourist destination and the High Street throngs with cars and people throughout the summer.

**5** A similar view of the same scene, but again from the 1950s and taken on the same day as the 1950s east-end picture. The *Marlborough Head* has a new sign and overhead wires have appeared, but the magnificent period buildings on the right are largely unchanged.

**6** The same stretch of Dedham High Street, from the opposite direction, *c.*1910. The building on the left with the gabled roof is Brook House, dating from at least the early 16th century and once owned by the prosperous Webbe family of clothiers. The Congregational Church on the right dates from the early 1870s and is now an art and craft centre. The trees in the distance mark the footpath to Flatford.

**7** St Mary's church, financed by local cloth merchants, dates from 1492-1519, before the collapse of the cloth industry. The open space to the left of the war memorial is known as Royal Square, its shape being dictated by the farmyard of the original manor house, which stood just outside the churchyard wall.

**8** The war memorial was erected by public subscription *c.*1920, to the designs of W.D. Caroe. This picture is thought to date from 1921 or 1922. The tributary quatrain on the memorial recalls the words of Captain Thomas James on an expedition to find the North West Passage.

**9** *(Left)* Church from the south east, *c.*1907. The present building replaced a smaller 14th-century church, which itself had replaced a Norman or Saxon structure. Caen stone from Normandy for the new building is thought to have been brought in on the nearby River Stour. There are some remains of the 14th-century building in the south porch doorway. The sender of this card, posted in 1907, writes that 'Auntie met us where the tram stopped'.

**10** *(Bottom Left)* A photograph of the magnificent interior of Dedham church, looking west, taken from a glass negative of *c.*1870 and showing the beautiful old box pews and high pulpit, which have since been removed.

**11** *(Below)* A later view of the church interior looking east. In 1967 the people of Dedham, Massachussetts, which had been founded by settlers from old Dedham families, including the prominent Sherman family, sent £1,000 for church restoration.

**12** *(Top Left)* A rare early view of Dedham High Street from the church tower, looking towards the Congregational Church, with Dedham Vale in the distance and the Royal Grammar School buildings in the right foreground. This card dates from the turn of the century, when Dedham was described as 'a small decayed town'—a planned railway had not been completed because of a fall in wheat prices in the 1870s. Note the absence of the war memorial in Royal Square—the horrors of war were still a decade away.

**13** *(Left)* The Royal Grammar School was founded in 1571, but this building dates from the 1730s. The school closed in 1889. A Fireworks Night bonfire for pupils was held in Royal Square until mid-Victorian times. The building later became The Old House Hotel. It was also once the studio of Sir Alfred Munnings, President of the Royal Academy. This photograph dates from *c.*1940.

**14** *(Above)* The *Marlborough Head* and the adjoining Loom House (extreme right) were originally one big building, used as a wool clearing house. The ground floor of the building had open sides and was used as a wool trading hall. The upper floors were for storage and there were dyeing vats in the cellars. After 1660, when the cloth trade was in decline, the corner building became an apothecary's shop. At about this time it was also used as an inn called *Tastours*. By 1704 it had become the *Marlborough Head*, named for the Duke of Marlborough, who defeated the French at Blenheim in that year. Loom House was once known as Church House and, before that, Cheese House, for its connection with the manor house dairy sheds which stood over the road in what is now Royal Square.

**15**  Mill Lane looking north. There were three main exits from Dedham churchyard—one in the east wall led to the manor house and two in the north wall led to the mill and the market respectively. This is a view from the churchyard exit to Mill Lane—the mill can be seen at the bottom of the hill in the distance. The *Marlborough Head* (right) had its timberwork plastered over at this stage, whilst the shop on the opposite corner, for a time known as Corner House, seems to be selling a variety of objects. It was variously a saddlers, stationers, hardware store and tearooms and the upper storey was originally overhanging. Both buildings are thought to date from at least the early 16th century.

**16**  A view of Mill Lane from the opposite direction, *c.*1905. Mill House (on the left) was the home of John Constable's sister, Martha, and her miller husband, Nathaniel Whalley. Staying there in 1821, Constable wrote of Dedham that 'I wish we had a small house here'.

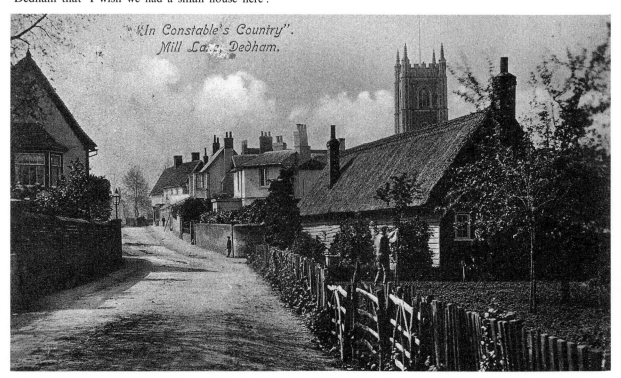

**17** Dedham High Street, west of Mill Lane—a picture taken specially for Smith's Stores, now the Co-operative grocers. William Smith operated a house furnishing business from the 1890s to *c*.1930. The corner shop is still selling a range of goods. The large building in the centre is Ivy House. Next to that is Sherman's.

**18** A close-up of Sherman's, which was given in 1599 by Edmund Sherman for use as an English School (for the teaching of English and Maths, rather than Greek and Latin grammar). The building itself dates from the 1730s. Descendants of the Sherman family found much fame and fortune in the New World, General W.T. Sherman being perhaps the most famous.

**19** The 16th-century *Sun Hotel* in Dedham High Street, looking back towards the *Marlborough Head*. Dedham market was held on this stretch, between the two pubs. In its heyday it was principally for wool and agricultural products and most of the buildings seen in this picture were owned by clothiers or had some cloth industry connection. The main market day was Tuesday, with business starting at 9am after an hour-long sermon in the churchyard opposite.

**20** The *Sun Hotel*, formerly *Bards*, was an important stopping point in the stagecoach era—hence the high archway into the yard from the High Street. The projecting building on the right hides a rare covered-staircase-cum-dovecote. The buildings on the left housed the stables—demolished by 1937. There was probably also a covered gallery. Before the Dedham Assembly Rooms were built, the *Sun* was a focal point for social events, notably as a before-and-after venue for bowls teams, whose matches took place across the road in the grounds of Albany Cottage.

**21** The *Sun Hotel, c.*1955. The old stagecoach archway (just visible on the extreme right) is now being used as the entrance to the carpark.

**22** The High Street, west of the *Sun Hotel, c.*1910. The red brick building on the extreme right is now called Dairy House. The ground-floor frontage of the building next to it has been altered and now houses a gift/flower shop and an estate agent's.

**23** High Street and 'Ye Olde Curiosity Shop', *c.*1910. This card was published for Major Charles Ray (Major was his name, not his rank), who ran a stationers, circulating library and 'fancy repository', *c.*1900-1930. He was also assistant overseer and parish clerk. The building in the background stands on the corner of Princel Lane, sometimes known as Compass or Compasses Lane after the inn on the opposite corner. The *Compasses Inn* lost its licence in 1912 and is now the Compasses Bookshop. The wrought iron inn sign was not, however, removed until the advent of double-decker buses. The name, Princel Lane, derives from the princely village green which gradually disappeared from this area as the town expanded. Many of the buildings in this picture were destroyed by fire in the late 1970s.

**24** A wonderful picture of the inside of Major Ray's shop. As the name over the door fortuitously implies, it was a veritable Aladdin's Cave. The pavement outside the shop was apparently equally well-stocked!

25  A rare photo of the grounds of Princel House, which lies at the bottom of Princel Lane.

26  Princel House was used for a time as a
'High Class Convalescent Home', though
unfortunately the exact date of this wonderful
advertisement is unknown.

**27** High Street, west of Princel Lane. Eley's bakers closed in 1984 after 90 years in business and this building is now home to a clothes shop and a dentist. All bread was baked on the premises until as recently as 1962, the method of delivery to neighbouring villages progressing from hand-cart to motorcycle. The next building now houses the offices of the well-known architects, Erith & Terry. Other buildings in this row once housed the telephone exchange and a private school.

**28** On the extreme left of this photo is Great House, erected in the 1930s to replace an earlier building of the same name which was destroyed by fire. Bricks found in the basement of the earlier building gave a date of 1678, though the building itself was from 1746. During the First World War, it was used as an organising depot.

# Dedham—Surrounds

**29** Entrance from the Colchester road, *c.*1905. The western end of Dedham village. The road on the right was the newer route to Colchester, but soon became more popular than the Brook Street route because it was more direct. The road on the left leads to Stratford St Mary. Its construction in 1523 was financed from the will of the clothier, John Webbe, to replace the old track along the river bank which emerged in Dedham next to Westgate House. The village lock-up, a square wooden building with oak louvres at the front, stood near the cottages on the right.

**30** A general view of Dedham, *c.*1950. The cottages from the previous picture can be seen on the right. Stratford Road disappears off to the left. The church, as always, dominates the scene.

**31** Shirburn Mill, *c*.1945, which stands at the extreme eastern end of Dedham parish.

# Dedham—Southfields

**32** Southfields (sometimes called the Flemish Houses or the Bay and Say Factory) was built in the late 15th or early 16th century for one of the wealthy Dedham clothier families. Its name derives from its position in the fields south of the old Dedham manor house. Built round a courtyard with an entrance to the north, it was never a cloth factory *per se*, but was rather the business residence, storehouse and offices of the clothier family.

**33** With the decline of the cloth industry, Southfields was divided into tenements, probably about 1800. This is the north-east corner, *c.*1905. The upper storey of the east range was originally one long room where finished cloth was stored before carting. The ground floor housed the cart sheds and equipment; the basement housed cellars and dyeing vats, giving access to the Black Brook for washing cloth and tenterframes in the meadows for stretching it. The two girls are Lily and Jessie Sage. In the background, Ede Hitchcock is talking to 'Donkey' Norman, whose cart was pulled not by a horse but by a donkey.

**34** With Castle House (now the Munnings' Art Museum) and Knights (in East Lane), Southfields was one of the most important cloth buildings in Dedham. Its special value today is in providing a rare example of the use for business of a building built round a quadrangle. The north side (pictured here) probably held the counting house and offices.

**35** The south-west corner of Southfields' courtyard, *c.*1920. The south-west wing was the most important part of the building as it was the residence of the clothier family. The writer of this card tells its recipient that 'we came here by charabanc'.

**36** Workhouse Corner, with Southfields in the distance and the old workhouse on the left. The two-storey section is the oldest part, dating from 1725. The single-storey section contained the Governor's house, plus offices and storage space. The workhouse closed in 1835, apparently in debt, and was converted into tenements by Mr. Whitmore Baker, the local vet. The frontage to Brook Street now bears the name Whitmore Place.

# Dedham—Mill & Lock

**37** There was a mill at Dedham in Saxon times and there have been at least three others on the site since then. The mills' main uses have been for fulling (cleaning and thickening) cloth and grinding corn. Constable painted one mill in 1820. This is a later building, seen about 1904.

**38**  At 11.30pm on Friday 19 June 1908 Dedham Mill caught fire. Local entrepreneurs were evidently quick to recognise the marketable potential of photographs of the event—this card was posted on 11 July!

**39**  The new mill, pictured *c.*1927. The sender of this card thought the mill that Constable 'was so fond of painting' to be 'an extremely ugly building'. Had they really seen the one Constable painted, they might have felt differently about it! This building was converted into flats in the late 1980s, with one section—Clover's Mill—being named after a previous owner. Percy Clover paid river tolls to Dedham until 1930. His last payment was 33 shillings.

**40** The original river crossing point at Dedham was a ford downstream from the current bridge by the mill. Mill Lane was diverted when the bridge was built. This is the old bridge, *c.*1903. The construction of one bridge at Dedham was delayed because the timber that was to be used was stolen by the poor for use as firewood!

**41** The mill pool, looking downriver towards a later bridge (this card was posted in 1923). The mill pool is today used for canoeing and pleasure boating. The mill itself is just out of the picture on the right.

**42** A close-up of Dedham Lock, looking upstream. The building on the right is the lock-keeper's cottage, now private property. This picture was taken *c.*1906 and one of the Stour barges, called 'lighters', can be seen just beyond the lock gates. This lock was restored by the River Stour Trust in 1990 and remains in full working order.

**43** A similar view of Dedham Lock, *c.*1920, giving a better view of the lock-keeper's cottage. The ditch on the right has now silted up.

**44** The Dedham lock-keeper and his wife, *c*.1905. The raised boarding at the back of the boat may have been designed to protect the occupants against rough water when rowing in the estuary.

**45** A rather ramshackle-looking Dedham Boathouse, *c*.1905. Boat hire is still popular here, though today's tourists tend to be a little less overdressed for the occasion!

# Dedham—Gun Hill Area

**46** Old toll-house and bridge, *c.*1909. The main London-Ipswich road originally passed through the extreme western end of Dedham parish. The tollbridge over the Stour at the bottom of Gun Hill joined Dedham to Stratford St Mary. It was a major route for through traffic and often featured in Constable's paintings. The building on the right is the toll-house. The building on the left with the tall chimney is now Le Talbooth restaurant, but has had several functions over the years (see no. **47**). The road here has been raised by a number of successive improvements—hence the buildings are lower than the road.

**47** A view of what is now Le Talbooth restaurant from the river. Originally called Leggs, it was the Tollbooth by 1659 when it comprised a mill-house, smith's shop and weighing building, in which waterborne goods were weighed so that tolls could be collected for the upkeep of the bridge (note the barge in the foreground). This picture shows it when it was the village lime kiln. A small house and other buildings on the site became known as Lime Kiln Cottages.

**48** Gun Hill was so steep that the road toll-house contained a 'Dumb Beasts' Petition'—a poem (now in nearby Langham church) instructing drovers to look after their animals when pulling carts uphill. When motorised transport arrived, it was going downhill that was the problem. Despite road straightening and the cutting away of part of the hill to reduce the gradient, there was still a dangerous bend to be negotiated. The toll-house was apparently demolished in a similar accident to this one. Even in this picture, the window and post box from the picture before last have been lost.

**49** Gun Hill Cottage, *c.*1905, which was demolished to make way for road widening.

# East Bergholt—Church Street

CONSTABLE'S BIRTHPLACE, EAST BERGHOLT.

**50**  Constable's birthplace, East Bergholt House, from a postcard for A.F. Hynard, who operated 'Constable's Tea Gardens'. The picture is based on the frontispiece to Constable's *English Landscape* mezzotints, which were first produced 1830-2. The house itself was demolished *c.*1840.

**51** Another card produced for 'Constable's Tea Gardens', showing the only remaining section of the fabric of East Bergholt House, the laundry and stables, *c.*1930. This is now a house called 'The Court'. The front railings of East Bergholt House also survive (see next picture).

**52** The railings between the two cars on the right are the original railings of East Bergholt House. A sign advertising 'Constable's Tea Gardens' can be seen next to the second car. The building on the extreme right is Little Court, which still stands, while the grass on the left is a remnant of the old village green, enclosed since Constable's day when a fair was held there. Behind the fence on the left is West Lodge (see no. **53**). In the distance is the Old Manse, where the earliest legal dissenters' meeting in Bergholt took place in 1689.

**53** The west front of West Lodge, from whose garden Constable painted many of his early views of Dedham Vale. It was renamed 'Stour' by Randolph Churchill—who wrote part of his biography to his father, Sir Winston, here.

**54** A view of Church Street from the opposite direction, with Little Court just out of the picture on the left. St Mary's church was one of Constable's most important early subjects, sketched more than any other building. The buildings on the left are almshouses, erected in 1896.

# East Bergholt—The Church

**55** An unusual text postcard, giving brief details of St Mary's.

**56** A close-up of the unfinished Wolsey Tower, referred to in the text card. Cardinal Wolsey dissolved several Suffolk priories, including nearby Dodnash Priory, to finance the building of colleges at Ipswich and Cambridge. Tradition has it that he wanted to make up for this by financing a church tower, but fell from grace before being able to complete it.

**57** Wolsey Tower from the opposite direction, looking back up Church Street towards the Manse, *c*.1920. Alternative theories for the non-completion of the tower are the collapse of the cloth trade or that, after the Reformation, wealthy people tended to leave money to the poor rather than to the Church. Even so, money was left in wills for the completion of the tower until at least as late as 1541. A Victorian plan for completion is on display inside the church.

**58** The church from the south west. The photographer is standing in Flatford Lane, which leads down to Flatford Mill. The building on the right is Churchgate House, which may once have been a guildhall of the religious guild of St John the Baptist. The memorial cross was designed by Mr. F.C. Eden, unveiled at a ceremony on 17 July 1921. The village stocks once stood by the church gate.

**59** A close-up of St Mary's porch, subject of a famous early Constable painting exhibited at the Royal Academy in 1810. There is a small priest's room above the doorway.

**60** The church from the south east, *c*.1910—one of a number of cards of East Bergholt produced by Fred and Frank Newell of Manningtree. The churchyard contains the bodies of Constable's parents, their doctor William Travis, Constable's friend John Dunthorne and the Flatford farmer, Willy Lott. Constable himself is buried at Hampstead. The earliest legible gravestone dates from 1693. The churchyard was closed for interments in 1854, when the new cemetery was inaugurated.

**61** This postcard of the interior of East Bergholt church is dated 1921, but it must be earlier because the chancel screen, which is not shown here, was dedicated by Bishop Dr. Hodgson in 1920. The east window shows five incidents in the life of Christ, plus the four evangelists and various Old Testament characters. The north chapel (on the left, behind the pillars) is now the vestry and organ chamber.

**62** A close-up of the chancel screen, designed by Sir T.G. Jackson and made by Messrs. Thompson & Son of Peterborough. Jackson also designed the choir stalls, reredos and marble flooring.

**63** The parish chest, dated by the horned lock-plate to *c.*1400. The lid was probably made from a hollowed-out poplar tree.

**64** The bell cage was erected *c*.1531 as a temporary measure while the tower was being built. It originally stood to the east of the church but was moved to the north side in the 17th century following complaints from Joseph Chaplin at Old Hall. The cage is not unique, but the method of ringing—the bells are swung directly by hand contact—probably is.

**65** The bells are left upright because they are not counter-balanced and it would be difficult to get them upside down without momentum. They are said to be the heaviest five bells currently being rung in England (about 4.5 tons).

# East Bergholt—The Abbey

St.Mary's Abbey,
East Bergholt.

**66**  St Mary's Abbey, from the church roof. The Abbey grew up on the site of Old Hall, the principal manor of East Bergholt, when a community of Benedictine nuns arrived from Winchester in 1856-7. During the Second World War it was occupied by the army; then, in 1946, it became a Franciscan friary. Since 1974 it has been occupied by the Unit One Suffolk Housing Association and has now regained its original name of Old Hall.

Abbey Cottage
E Bergholt

**67** A close-up of Abbey Cottage, which stood near the entrance to the Abbey. The open space in front of it, called Church Plain, was the site of a market which probably sold food and provisions rather than goods connected with the cloth trade. The cottage has since been demolished.

**68** The Abbey from the south west, *c.*1962. The original Old Hall manor house is long gone, but its 18th-century successor—the building with the columned porch—survives. The tall tower, and numerous other extensions, were added by the nuns.

**69** Abbey novitiate detail, *c.*1925, with the figure of Christ. In 1909 the Abbey was rocked by scandal when one of the nuns, Margaret Mary Moult, 'escaped' from the strict regime that operated there. She was pursued to Manningtree station, where she finally found freedom. She wrote in her autobiography (*The Escaped Nun*) of 'enduring for seven years a life upon which I cannot look back even now without shuddering'.

**70** The Abbey chapel, showing the screen which was removed after the nuns left. The lay chapel, through the arches on the right, was opened at times to members of the public during both the Benedictine and Franciscan residencies. It is now sometimes used for public exhibitions.

St. Mary's Abbey, East Bergholt, Refectory.

**71** The nun's refectory is still used as the kitchen and dining area by members of the Unit One Suffolk Housing Association, but it now has a mezzanine floor at the end shown here.

**72** The abbey grounds, *c.*1930, looking towards the church. It was from the grounds of Old Hall that Constable painted some of his early westward views of Dedham Vale.

# East Bergholt—Rectory Hill

**73** The Old Chapel House, between the church and Rectory Hill, with Church Plain in the distance. It was never a chapel; the name is more likely to derive from the surname of a previous owner—the naming of houses in this fashion was an old Suffolk custom. The facade dates from 1818, but the rest of the building is probably much older.

Rectory Hill,
East Bergholt

**74** *(Above left)* Rectory Hill. The building in the foreground is now sub-divided into Rectory Hill Cottages but was originally one large house. It is thought to date from the early 16th century and there is evidence inside that it was once a cloth workshop. The shopfront extension has now disappeared. The other building is Hill House. The facade dates from 1836, but the structure behind it is older.

**75** *(Left)* At the bottom of Rectory Hill is Gissings, another 16th-century clothier's house with an early 19th-century facade. It takes its name from a previous owner. To the extreme left of the picture, attached to Gissings, is Ribblesdale, probably named after the Ryber stream.

**76** *(Above)* A close-up of Gissings.

**77** The Old Rectory, *c*.1910. In 1714 Reverend Edward Alston moved the rectory from Flatford to the building now called 'The Old Rectory' on Rectory Hill. It was much enlarged in the 1820s, but was itself replaced in 1904 by the building now known as Emmanuel House. The Old Rectory was known for some years as 'Woodcote', the name it bears on this picture.

# East Bergholt—
# The Street and Gaston Street

**78** The *Red Lion*, formerly the *Lion*, where Church Street meets The Street. The building obscured by the pub's single-storey extension is the Old Manse. The small building on the right in the background was Constable's first studio, bought by his father in 1802. The building on the extreme left is now an estate agents. The petrol pumps have gone and the flat-roofed building in front of Constable's old studio is now the village post office. On the extreme right is Red Lion Cottage, which was restored in the 1980s and now sports exposed timber framing. It was originally two cottages.

**79** Opposite the *Red Lion* is the single-storey 'Hatters', which still displays the ancient wall-sign 'Dealer in Hatts'. Straw hats were made in East Bergholt well into Victorian times.

**80** Green's Stores in 1930. The shop stood on the inside of the bend just beyond 'Hatters'. Mr. Lebell, the manager, is on the right; next to him is Mrs. East. The building on the left is now Fountain House Stores; the main building is Stour Crafts. The roof of Fountain House itself, which Mrs. Green lived in, can been seen top right.

**81** In the opposite direction were the old post office-cum-telephone exchange and Barclays Bank. The post office, said to have been closed because of a failure to deliver a telegram on New Year's Day, is now the pharmacy, while the bank is now a private house called Wren Cottage. The village pound stood to the extreme right of this picture, where De'Aths bakery now stands. The bakery was Mr. Wilderspin's pharmacy in the 1930s.

**82** Just beyond this row of buildings The Street becomes Gaston Street, which was largely undeveloped until Victorian times. The gaps between the few old houses that survived have now been filled with comparatively modern development, giving a wide variety of styles.

**83** Gaston House was built *c*.1840, though it looks as if it might be older. This picture dates from about 1908.

**84** Further up Gaston Street are these three buildings—Wistaria Cottage, Wanstead and Woodford. Wistaria Cottage is one of a number of early 19th-century brick buildings in this vicinity. This is clearly an early photograph, though the exact date in unknown.

**85** Two interesting buildings further up Gaston Street, *c*.1925. The one in the foreground is here called 'The Poplars', but is now known as Marton House. The one behind is Richardsons (see no. **86**).

**86** A later view of a very different looking Richardsons—on the right, with timber frame now exposed. In 1851 there were only 16 houses in Gaston Street from Tufnells at one end to Gothics at the other. Most of them were in this vicinity, near Richardsons Farm.

**87** Cottages at Gaston End. This scene has changed a great deal.

# East Bergholt—Public Houses

**88** Burnt Oak, based around the *King's Head*, was one of the 'Ends'—the satellite hamlets to the main East Bergholt village. The building on the right was called the Town House and was bought by the parish overseers in 1654 to house the poor. It is now divided into private residences. The buildings on the left probably date from the 16th century.

**89** The same road from the opposite direction, *c.*1910. The house in the centre has since been replaced.

**90** 'Sixer' was one of Bergholt's best-known characters. This photograph was taken outside the *King's Head*, which was apparently his 'local'.

**91** Tarbin's Corner on the Gaston Street/B1070 junction at Gaston End. The *Carriers Arms* (out of sight on the left) was first listed in 1881 and may well have grown up on the site of a carrier's yard. The main building in this picture, Jessupp & Tarbin's shop, is now known as Stuarts. It dates from the 16th century. The building on the extreme right is the *Beehive Inn*.

**92** A wonderful close-up of the *Beehive Inn*, showing several early 20th-century Bergholt characters. The man on the tricycle is thought to be Mr. A. Hurrell. Second from the right is probably Mr. K. Bedwell; fourth from the right, a Mr. Underwood.

**93**   White Horse Road. The *White Horse* originally stood on the corner of Bergholt Heath at Baker's End, but was moved to what is now White Horse Road around the turn of the century. That replacement pub (centre) is now a house, while the single-storey buildings on the left have been replaced.

# East Bergholt—Surrounds

**94** Manningtree Road—now the busy B1070 Heath Road at Gaston End—*c.*1911. The thatched cottage has gone, but the other two buildings survive. The one on the left is divided into two cottages—Gascoignes and Chaplins. The fence in the distance has been replaced by a distinctive red brick wall.

**95** *(Below)* Ackworth House, shown here in about 1905, was built *c.*1780-90. In 1838 what was thought to be a Roman burial ground was dug up in this vicinity and apparently Roman earthworks are still visible in the grounds. The grounds themselves cover 50 acres and contain three cottages. The property was once in the ownership of the de Zoete family, of Barclays de Zoete Wedd fame.

**96** *(Right)* Another view of Ackworth House, showing the south front which affords wonderful views over the Stour Valley. The conservatory on the left has now disappeared.

**97** *(Bottom right)* Dodnash Lodge, East Bergholt. Dodnash Priory was dissolved by Cardinal Wolsey *c.*1524-5.

**98** The old Methodist Chapel, now demolished. The stone bearing its erection date is thought to be languishing in a local garden.

**99** The Mission Room at East End, the most remote of Bergholt's satellite hamlets.

# Flatford—Approach

The Road to Flatford

**100** Flatford Lane, just below East Bergholt church. The wall on the right marked the boundary of the grounds of Old Hall.

**101** Tunnel Lane, Flatford, so called because the trees close over it from both sides. Its appearance has been preserved by the purchase of land at Haybarn Cottage on the left and, on the right, the riverside field that was once rented out by Dedham-based painter, Sir Alfred Munnings.

**102** Hay Barn, at the top of Tunnel Lane. Speculation that there was once a church at Flatford is largely based on William Brasier's map of 1731, which shows an 'Old Parsonage' just above Hay Barn and a 'Church Field' to the west of Valley Farm (see no. **119**).

# Flatford—Bridge Cottage and Bridge

**103** The first building encountered at the bottom of Tunnel Lane is Bridge Cottage, owned by the National Trust since 1985 but formerly operated privately as a tearoom. The cottage contains an exhibition of the life of John Constable, whose most important paintings featured scenes at Flatford.

104   Flatford Bridge, *c*.1890. The pastime of watching the river from the bridge is evidently at least a century old.

105   Bridge Cottage and Bridge from the Essex side, *c*.1936 (though technically the county boundary follows the old river, some distance behind the photographer). The trees on the right have gone and a boat-hire company now operates from the opposite bank. This is one of a series of cards of Flatford by Cook & Eaves of Clacton.

**106** The interior of Bridge Cottage, showing the fireplace in the principal downstairs room.

**107** Bridge Cottage and the dry dock, *c*.1920. On the riverbank to the right of Bridge Cottage is a dry dock where barges were repaired. Featured in Constable's painting, 'Boatbuilding' (1814), it was recently rediscovered and restored in a joint operation between the National Trust and the River Stour Trust.

Bridge and Cottage, Flatford.

# Flatford—The Lock

108 Flatford Lock, looking upstream towards Bridge Cottage, c.1900. Constable painted several lock pictures and even appeared before the Commissioners of the Stour Navigation on behalf of his father (who operated Flatford Mill) to protest about the state of the lock and towpath.

109 The original turf-sided lock that Constable knew was slightly to the north of the existing one. It can be seen here to the left of the barge in this picture of c.1905. It was replaced c.1840 by the wood-sided lock seen here, which was itself refitted with concrete sides in the 1930s.

**110** A close-up of the wood-sided lock, some time before 1930. Note the state of the towpath and the millpool beyond the lock.

**111** Another close-up of the same lock in 1938. The wooden sides have been replaced by concrete ones and the towpath and millpool have been improved, the work being done by the South Essex Waterworks Company, who wanted to use the river for abstraction purposes. The lock was fully restored by the River Stour Trust in 1991-2. The chimneys in the background are on Flatford Mill.

# Flatford—Principal Buildings

JOHN·CONSTABLE·R·A·1776-1837

Leonard R. Squirrell, R.E.

**Flatford Mill**

(Suffolk)

Presented to the Nation by Mr. & Mrs. T. R. Parkington

September 8th, 1928

**112** By the 1920s, concern was being expressed about the derelict state of some of the buildings at Flatford and a campaign to save them was set in motion. In 1927, following an appeal, much of the Flatford Mill Estate was bought for the nation by Thomas Parkington of Ipswich. This card commemorates that event.

**113** Flatford Mill and mill pool. The present Flatford Mill is thought to date from around 1730, but there was a mill on the site long before that. It was described as 'ruinous' in 1689 and is recorded as existing in the 14th century. The old river was diverted to its present course to raise the water level so that milling could take place. Like Dedham, its main uses have been for fulling cloth and grinding corn. The mill was home to the Constable family from 1765 to 1774, when they moved to East Bergholt House. It remained the family's business premises until the 1840s and closed in 1901. It was acquired by the National Trust from the estate of Thomas Parkington in 1943 and is now leased to the Field Studies Council.

**114** Flatford Mill from the north east, showing the mill stream overflow which was the site of Constable's most famous painting, 'The Haywain' (1821). Willy Lott's Cottage is behind the photographer.

**115** Flatford Mill from Willy Lott's Cottage (dating from *c.*1600 and on the left). The cottage looks as if it has seen better days and it was the poor condition of this building which prompted the 1920s campaign to save Flatford.

**116** A view in the opposite direction, looking towards Willy Lott's Cottage from the mill. When Lott lived here it was actually called Gibeon's Farm, probably from the Gobione family. Constable's pictures, however, made the building so famous that it is now named after its former owner. Nearby Gibbonsgate Lake retains a link with the old name.

**117** Willy Lott's Cottage from the classic 'Haywain' viewpoint. Judging from its appearance, this picture probably dates from the 1920s, when the estimated cost of repairing the building was £1,750. A 1925 report stated: 'The house has suffered severely from neglect of recent years. The tiles are off the gable end of the East Wing; the external plaster is either off or on the point of falling; the beam which formed the head of the principal fireplace has been removed, and the brickwork above is falling and endangers the whole stack. The first floor has been taken out from the west end of the house and some of the ground floor rooms have been stripped of their floor pavings... If it is to be saved, action must be taken very soon, for decay is now becoming very rapid—there will not be much left in 15 or 20 years if it is not taken in hand now.'

**118** A rear view of Willy Lott's Cottage, *c.*1938. Its condition has noticeably improved.

**119** Valley Farm (Flatford Manor House). Constable sometimes referred (incorrectly) in his painting titles to Willy Lott's Cottage as being 'Valley Farm'. This is the real Valley Farm, the original Flatford manor house. It was owned for many years by the Richardson family, who also operated the tearooms at Bridge Cottage. It was acquired by the National Trust in 1959 and is the residence of the Field Studies Council's Director of Studies.

**120** Valley Farm outbuildings, *c*.1908.

# The River

**121** Constable's journey to school took him across Fen Bridge—his favourite part of the journey. The original bridge collapsed sometime around the 1930s and was replaced in 1985 at a cost of £14,000. It had to be flown in by helicopter because of the lack of road access. This card was produced for Dedham stationer, Major Charles Ray, probably in the 1920s.

**122** Fen Bridge from the opposite direction, showing farmhands at work in the fields. The river was used for transporting agricultural produce to market. Much of this land is now owned by the National Trust.

**123** Barges coupled together, *c.*1900-5. Stour barges, called 'lighters', were usually towed in pairs by a single horse. Once they reached the river estuary, however, it was not possible to use horses, so several pairs were coupled together. This photo shows two pairs in the estuary below Brantham.

**124** A barge negotiating Flatford Lock, *c.*1905, with a good view of the towing horse and minder. Note the tow-rope leading from the horse into the water.

**125** Transporting the horse, *c.*1905. The towpath on the Stour crossed the river several times, so the horse pulling the barges had to be ferried across to the opposite bank at regular intervals. This photo shows this process taking place.

**126** Man catching eels, *c.*1900. Catching eels was once a popular pastime on the Stour, as this photo shows. The location is below Flatford Mill, where the water was tidal.

**127** The River, showing Dedham church.

**128** Cows and pollarded willows are still two of the main features of the riverbank. Sir Alfred Munnings felt so strongly about maintaining the willows, which were used for making fence poles, that he once paid for them to be repollarded. 'Year by year,' he wrote, 'they split and fall apart, a desolate scene of wreckage, with cattle rubbing in the skeleton branches on the meadows.'

129 River Stour, Dedham. A peaceful and timeless view of the river.

**130**  A river outing at Dedham Lock. The artist is Thomas Pyne, who painted a lot of local views. The trees on the right are long gone, but taking a pleasure cruise on the river is still possible, thanks to the River Stour Trust's 'Stour Trusty'. The more energetic can hire rowing boats from just beyond the bridge.

**131**  Dedham boy scouts on a river outing in the 1920s as part of the annual 'Beating the Bounds' ceremony. Such ceremonies elsewhere involved walking the length of the parish boundary. At Dedham, where part of the boundary was the river, this would have been impractical. The man at the back right is Ted Eley, a member of the famous Eley bakery family.

# Neighbouring Villages

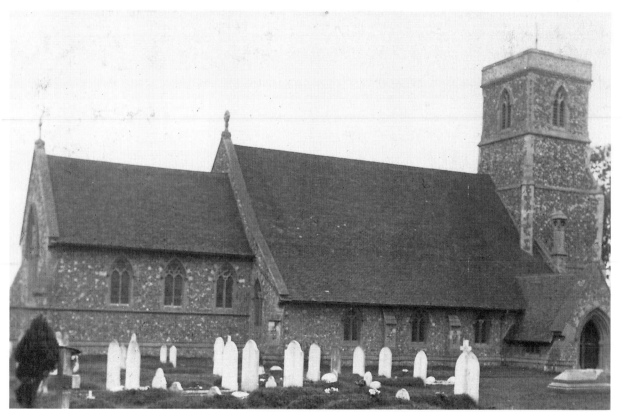

**132** Brantham church. East Bergholt parish was joined with Brantham until 1855, when Reverend Joshua Rowley left the advowson to Emmanuel College, Cambridge (his old college). Rowley was buried in the chancel at Brantham because he died on 28 December 1854, three days before East Bergholt churchyard closed for burials. Brantham church was home to one of only three religious works by Constable. The original is now in Emmanuel College but the church displays a copy.

**133** Brantham church, lychgate and street. The lychgate was designed by the late Victorian architect, E.S. Prior. The building in the background is now used by a children's playgroup and there is a row of single-storey houses to its immediate right.

**134** The current Brantham rectory was built in 1932. This is its predecessor, *c.*1924. The building is now a private house called Brantham Glebe.

**135** The River Stour estuary below Brantham. There is evidence that the ancient farming community of bell-beaker people once lived at Brantham. Certainly the village's position on the estuary would have made it an important early settlement area.

**136** British Xylonite Company order form, 1928. The British Xylonite Company came to Brantham in 1887 and subsequently became one of the area's largest employers. Xylonite, a product similar to celluloid, was used in combs, toys and musical instruments. The company bought land at Brooklands Farm for its factory and provided 60 new houses and other facilities for its workers, giving the area 'the characteristics of a model industrial village'. The company is now Wardle Storeys.

**137** New Village, Brantham, shown here *c.*1911, was built to house the workers of the British Xylonite Company. The houses survive with minor changes, but the fields at the end of the road have been opened up to form Brooklands Road.

**138** The church at Stratford St Mary, *c.*1910, which stands on the opposite side of the valley from Dedham church. Constable was familiar with this building and sketched it from several angles.

**139** Higham church, thought to be the building depicted in Constable's 'The Cornfield' (1826). It has been much restored but retains some 13th-century features.

# People

**140** Dedham boy scouts going off to camp.

**141** Dedham School pupils. Note the soles of the boys' boots. Unfortunately the date on the slate is not discernible.

**142** An all-girl class from Dedham School in 1911.

**143** Mrs Land's lace class. The class made costumes for local productions of 'The Mikado', 'The Japanese Fan' and 'A Midsummer Night's Dream'.

**144** Dedham cricket team in 1935.

**145** Staff at Eley's Bakery in Dedham High Street, *c.*1930. The Eley family also owned Dedham boatyard and had a tearoom where Barclays Bank now stands.

**146** Canon G.H. Rendall in the vicarage garden, *c.*1935. Rendall wrote several books about Dedham.

**147** Miss Dunnet, seen here about to climb into her carriage, lived in a big house on the outskirts of Dedham. She is buried in Dedham churchyard. The coachman is Ted Daughters.

**148** The Folkard family ran the *Carrier's Arms* in East Bergholt around the turn of the century. This is William—one of three sons—who was a hawker in East Bergholt, Great Wenham, Capel St Mary, Copdock and Washbrook, where this picture was taken in 1910. The other sons became the village baker and the postman at Brantham. Folkard was probably an old cloth family name. Francis Folkard was involved with the building of Burnt Oak School in 1831.

**149**  Edward Rampling was an East Bergholt butcher and a well-known figure in the village. This photograph shows him with his mother and was apparently taken in the Ramplings' garden.

**150**  Frank Smith's saddler's and harnessmaker's in Heath Road, East Bergholt. Smith probably took the shop over from John Bloom, who was trading there in the 1870s and 1880s. He was a well-known local Methodist preacher.

**151**  Mr. & Mrs. Double. James Double was a coke and coal merchant and a carter in East Bergholt. In 1888 he was also a farm bailiff.

**152** The tar men, apparently at Tarbin's Corner, East Bergholt, in the 1920s. Left to right: Mr. Prettiman Clark; Arty Lilly; F. Peck; Reid the horseman.

**153** East Bergholt choir and clergy outside their church.

No. 13 PLATOON, 4th VOLUNTEER BATT. SUFFOLK REGIMENT.

EAST BERGHOLT, 1915—1919.

R. C. Hammond, G. S. Leeks, C. Lawrence, C. E. Cresswell, W. J. Everitt, J. Barnes, F. L. Buckles, F. W. Rose, Cpl. G. Norfolk, H. H. Noel, W. J. Rose.
C. Duckling, L.-cpl. T. Clifton, F. V. Packard, L.-cpl. F. Goodchild, H. H. Paskell, L. Barton, E. B. K. Norman, A. J. Bedwell, W. Gardiner, W. J. Tedder.
L. Richardson, W. Brooke, Cpl. E. Clark, Sergt. G. Adcock, Pltn. Sergt F. A. Hicks, Capt. G. Milbank, 2nd Lt. J. G. Robertson, C Q M S. Green, J. R. Francis, A. Lawrence, J. B. Richardson.
Cpl. B. W. Bennett, F. T. Mitchell, L. C. W. Smith, G. White, C. J. Stoggles, H. J. Ablitt, W. G. Song r, W. Stiff, Cpl. H. W. Tedder.

**154** No. 13 Platoon, 4th Volunteer Battalion, Suffolk Regiment, East Bergholt, 1915-19, complete with names. Many of these men came from old Bergholt families.

**155** The Xylonite Works Prize Band in about 1907. Such was the community spirit at Brantham's prosperous xylonite factory that social activities were always well supported. The band was said 'to supply entertainment in the winter evenings and is in request for garden parties, etc., in the summer'.

156 A marvellous picture of the boys of Burnt Oak School, East Bergholt, which first opened for business in 1831.

157 A nicely posed photo of the East Bergholt football team, *c.1919. Back row (left to right)*: H.A. Goodchild, C. Parker, Bill Conway, G. Tatum, ? Trainer; *Middle row (left to right)*: Edgar Attfield, Ray Hicks, Bill Moss; *Front row (left to right)*: G. Parker, Ken Wheeler, P. Roper, Bill Lloyd, Charlie Lloyd. Note that the player front right is smoking!

# Transport

**158** One of the lorries from Clover's Mill, Dedham, *c.*1935. The Clovers were the last family to operate Dedham Mill.

**159** Another Clover's lorry, plus workmen, *c.*1930. This picture was taken at Lamb Corner, Dedham.

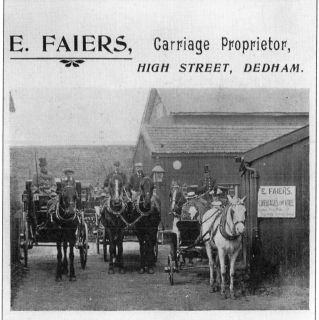

E. FAIERS, Carriage Proprietor,

*HIGH STREET, DEDHAM.*

**Landau, Broughams, Waggonettes, and Covered Carriages for Hire.**

**Any train can be met at Ardleigh or Manningtree on notice by wire or postcard.**

**160** An advertisement for E. Faiers, carriage proprietor. The business operated from Dedham High Street, opposite Princel Lane.

**161**  Two buses from Beeston's bus company, a well-known local outfit which operated in East Bergholt and the surrounding area. The company was later absorbed into the Eastern Counties bus company.

**162**  H. Butcher was another well-known bus company operating in and around East Bergholt. This picture, dating from *c.*1918, apparently shows some kind of outing—note the wonderful array of hats, particularly on the ladies. The driver is thought to be Harry Butcher's father.

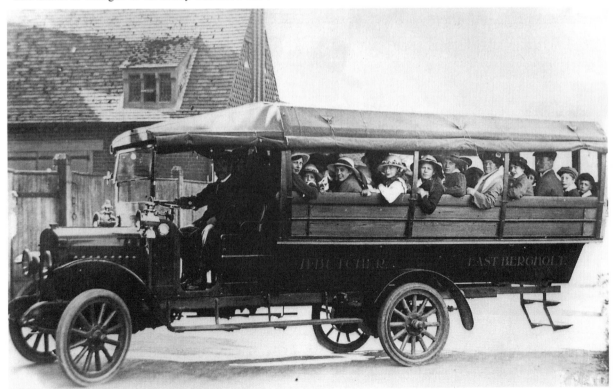

**163** The Moss family ran a taxi firm in East Bergholt. Mrs. Dorothy Moss used to drive, as, apparently, did a Mrs. Rogers, who is pictured here at the wheel.

**164** East Bergholt's Alan Wheeler, some time around the First World War. The make of bike is not clear, but note the unusual rounded petrol tank, the belt drive to the rear wheel, the foot rests and the side-valve engine, which appears to form part of the frame.

# Events

**165 & 166** Two marvellous side-by-side photographs of a service at the war memorial in Royal Square, Dedham, in 1922. Every vantage point is taken for a view of the event. The building on the left of Mill Lane behind the corner shop has since been destroyed by fire.

**167** Another big event in Royal Square, with the meeting of the hunt (known as The Meet) in 1911. Note the humble appearance of Smith's Stores compared with the previous two pictures. The steps of Sherman's (background left) are filled with schoolchildren, perhaps waiting for school to open. The small girl in the left foreground is Connie Eley, another member of the locally famous bakery family.

**168** A rare photograph of Dedham in the snow, supposedly taken on Christmas Day in the late 1930s.

**169** Three photographs from the Colchester Motorcycle Club speed trial in Long Road, Dedham, in 1913. The first shows what is presumably the line-up of competitors, before the commencement of the flying start, half-mile event.

**170** A competitor in action, with specially widened and flattened handlebars.

**171** Probably the winners, with what looks like the starter on the left (note the starting pistol, clipboard and armband). The machine on the right is a Rudge; in the middle is a TT-type Zenith-Gradua with overhead valve JAP engine; on the left a TT-type Triumph. The Zenith-Gradua rider is probably Mark Head, who won the Tourist Trophy and 1,000cc classes.

**172** Jim Eley, John Bradley and Bill Borley digging ARP trenches behind what is now the butcher's shop in Dedham High Street, *c.*1940.

173 The River Stour used to flood regularly around Flatford, as can be seen here. The river's level is now controlled, but the alteration to its original course meant that the adjacent fields were lower than the water. Floodwater often drained onto them and, in cold conditions, froze. Sir Alfred Munnings once painted a picture of his wife and some friends skating on one such frozen field.

174 On 15 June 1938 Queen Mary visited the Flatford Mill Estate to witness the efforts that had been made to preserve the buildings there. She is shown here (white dress) at Willy Lott's Cottage.

**175** Incendiary bombs dropped on East Bergholt from a German airship during the First World War.

**176** A marvellous photograph of the children from Burnt Oak School on VE Day, 1945. Note the poster on the bonfire, which invites locals to 'Come and see Hitler burnt tonight on the Gandish Meadows'.

# Select Bibliography

Booker, J., *Essex & the Industrial Revolution,* 1974
*Constable's Country—Pictorial and Historical, c.*1908-1918
Cornish, H., *The Constable Country—A Hundred Years After John Constable,* 1932
East Bergholt Society, *Victorian East Bergholt,* 1986
Edwards, R., *The River Stour,* 1982
Gallifant, P. (Ed.), *Dedham Vale Society—1938-88,* 1988
Gamlin, B., *Old Hall, East Bergholt,* 1990
Godwin, G.N., *Bits About Bergholt,* 1874
Jones, C.A., *History of Dedham,* 1907
Leslie, C.R., *Memoirs of the Life of John Constable,* 1843
Munnings, A., *The Finish,* 1952
Palmer, T., *Discover the Lower Stour,* 1992
Parris, L. & Fleming-Williams, I., *Constable,* 1991
Paterson, T.F., *East Bergholt in Suffolk,* 1923
Pluckwell, G., *John Constable's Essex,* 1987
Rendall, G.H., *Dedham in History,* 1937
Rendall, G.H., *Dedham, Described and Deciphered,* 1937
Rickword, G.O., *Constable's Country,* 1953
Rogers, N.G., *The Valley of the Stour,* 1992
*Royal Commission on Historical Monuments,* 1922
*Victoria County History*

Various publications by the Dedham Vale Society, the East Bergholt Society, the National Trust, the River Stour Trust and other local organisations, plus parish church guides and relevant newspaper and magazine sources held by the Essex and Suffolk Record Offices

# Index

Roman numerals refer to pages in the introduction and arabic numerals to individual illustrations.